EFFECTIVE
SPIRITUAL WARFARE

Other Snapshot Series Books

People, Trees and Poverty
A Snapshot of Environmental Missions

Lowell Bliss (Author)

People, Trees & Poverty shares a high-level overview of what it looks like to reach the unreached through advocacy on environmental issues. However, this book does more than raise awareness and pluck your heartstrings. It concludes with a critical feature, listing additional resources, gatherings, and organizations to move the reader from concern to action.

It's Your Call
To a Missional or Missionary Life

David P. Jacob (Author)

For most believers, several factors influence their missions call. Some are called to stay in their hometown and support missions at their local church, others are called to short-term mission trips, while others are called to spend a lifetime overseas. *It's Your Call* highlights three things that can help you discover the adventure God has for you in his mission: prayer and Bible study, missionary mentorship, and short-term mission trips.

Insiders and Alongsiders
An Invitation to the Conversation

Kevin Higgins (Author)

In *Insiders and Alongsiders*, Kevin Higgins offers his evolving perspective on "insider" movements (IMs), a controversial type of movement in which families and friendship networks become faithful followers of Jesus while remaining identified with the culture of their people group.

EFFECTIVE SPIRITUAL WARFARE

Wrestling in God's Strength

MARY LOU CODMAN-WILSON

Effective Spiritual Warfare: Wrestling in God's Strength

© 2022 by Mary Lou Codman-Wilson. All rights reserved.

No part of this book may be reproduced, stored in a retrieval system, or transmitted in any form or by any means—electronic, mechanical, photocopy, recording, or otherwise—without prior written permission from the publisher, except brief quotations used in connection with reviews in magazines or by permission. All rights reserved.

All Scripture quotations, unless otherwise indicated, are taken from the Holy Bible, New International Version®, NIV®. Copyright ©1973, 1978, 1984, 2011 by Biblica, Inc.™ Used by permission of Zondervan. All rights reserved worldwide. www.zondervan.com. The "NIV" and "New International Version" are trademarks registered in the United States Patent and Trademark Office by Biblica, Inc.™

Scripture quotations marked (NASB) are taken from the Amplified® Bible (AMP), Copyright © 2015 by The Lockman Foundation. Used by permission. www.lockman.org.

Scripture quotations marked (MSG) are taken from THE MESSAGE, copyright © 1993, 2002, 2018 by Eugene H. Peterson. Used by permission of NavPress, represented by Tyndale House Publishers. All rights reserved.

Scripture quotations marked (Passion Translation) are from The Passion Translation®. Copyright © 2017, 2018, 2020 by Passion & Fire Ministries, Inc. Used by permission. All rights reserved. ThePassionTranslation.com.

Published by William Carey Publishing
10 W. Dry Creek Cir
Littleton, CO 80120 | www.missionbooks.org

William Carey Publishing is a ministry of Frontier Ventures
Pasadena, CA | www.frontierventures.org

Cover and Interior Designer: Mike Riester

The Snapshot Series: Number 4

ISBNs: 978-1-64508-458-7 (paperback), 978-1-64508-460-0 (epub)

Printed Worldwide

26 25 24 23 22   1 2 3 4 5   IN

Contents

1. The Reality of the Spirit World	1
2. How Jesus Describes Satan	7
Accuser	7
Liar	9
Destroyer	11
3. Eight Ways Believers Can Win Victory against the Enemy	13
Submit to God	14
Put on God's Armor	17
Resist the Enemy	19
Quote Scripture	21
Sing and Praise	27
Pray as a Prayer Warrior	28
Claim God's Ability to Demolish Strongholds	30
Wrestle in God's Strength	31
Bibliography	32
Get Involved	33
Also by Dr. Mary Lou Codman-Wilson	34

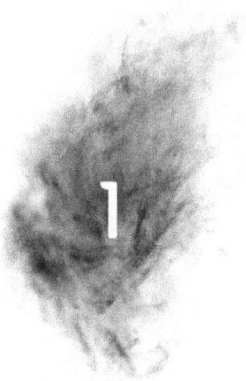

The Reality of the Spirit World*

The Bible makes it clear that the world we live in has both a material aspect—what can be seen and felt and proven by science and the senses—and an unseen spiritual world, where there is a great battle going on between the forces of God and the forces of evil. Jesus himself spoke often of Satan as the devil, the ruler of this world, a liar, an accuser, an enemy of God. Paul warned the Ephesian Christians,

> Put on the full armor of God, so that you can take your stand against the devil's schemes. For our struggle is not against flesh and blood, but against the rulers, against the authorities, against the powers of this dark world and against the spiritual forces of evil in the heavenly realms. (Eph 6:11–12)

John White in his classic book, *The Fight*, agrees with this biblical perspective. He says,

> When you became a Christian, a number of extremely important events took place both in heaven and in your own body. ... Justification, Regeneration—i.e., God imparting to you His own

---

* The material in this Snapshot book was adapted and expanded from chapter 17 of *Supracultural Gospel: Bridging East and West* (Littleton, CO: William Carey Publishing, 2022).

life ... and a new relationship with the powers of darkness. ... You are now the sworn foe of the legions of hell [This theme weaves throughout his entire book. He stresses it again in the very last chapter.] To acknowledge Jesus as Savior and Lord is to join an army. Whether you know it or not, you are enlisted.[1]

White describes the cosmic battle all Christians are engaged in as between Jesus Christ—the "UnConquerable One" and Satan—the "Infernal Majesty." White makes clear that God's victory is sure: "The battle is the Lord's." He also explains how this battle affects the Christian's prayer life, relationships, holiness, faith, and witness.

Globally, materialists and secularists only acknowledge the material aspect of reality. Included in that group are many from the Western world who dismiss the existence of the spirit world as well. But millions of other people, both Christians and nonbelievers, understand and confront the spirit world every day. David Hesselgrave says,

> This supernatural worldview includes deities and spirit beings of all kinds, good and evil. They are usually capricious and capable of being cajoled and influenced, especially by those individuals who are privy to the "right" rituals, incantations and "medicine." The spirits of departed ancestors are of special importance. ... They tend to be approachable and beneficent and are therefore the subject of regular and special rites and prayers. Quite often a "high god" exists, but in spite of his position, he is distant and does not receive the attention accorded to the gods and spirits who are closer in daily existence.[2]

---

[1] White, *The Fight*, 1-5, 169, 176.

[2] Hesselgrave, *Communicating Christ Cross-Culturally*, 228.

The Reality of the Spirit World

Believers need to understand the reality of the spirit world and learn how to fight against its destructive power in their lives and their countries. Therefore, a thorough introduction to effective spiritual warfare is a necessity for them. It will help them focus on the extent of Christ's victory over Satan. In Calvin Miller's book *The Singer*, he describes the cosmic conflict between Jesus and Satan in allegorical form. It is excerpted here in the poetic style of the entire book:

"Stop," cried a voice within the crowd, "You are still mad," the voice continued as the Hater came out of the crowd. "Listen to me, Madman," he said, pulling out the silver pipe.

Beads of perspiration appeared upon the Madman's brow. Fear tore at him—could he withstand the melody that formerly had driven him insane? The weird progression of shrieking notes began.

But the Madman's tension soon began to ease. In the frustration of losing, the Hater played more loudly than before.

Soon the Madman was entirely at peace. He exulted in the confidence of total sanity. "It's no use, Hater, the Troubadour has come."

The crowd had grown to several hundred people and the Madman called out over them, "This man's pipe wiped out all my sanity until today. I learned a new song from the Singer for whom the world so long has waited. Listen to the Song of Life."

He began to sing. The Singer himself was startled at the beauty of his voice. He sang with such confidence that none could doubt the meaning he found springing up within his soul.

"Where did you learn this confidence and joy?" they asked him.

He nodded toward the Singer. "He has saved me from myself and from a thousand maddened spirits from the Canyon of the Dammed."

"Who are you, Man?" they asked the Singer. "I am the Troubadour, the Son of Earthmaker," the Singer then replied. "I have come to save the world and close the Canyon of the Damned."[3]

One young believer in Christ tells of this encounter with evil at her parents' home in China:

> Recently I flew back to China to visit my family during winter break from my studies in the US. My parents had just moved into their new apartment and I stayed with them there. One day it was dark and raining. I was alone in the apartment when I felt an unexplainable sense of fear rise from my heart. I felt that there was something/someone in my room. My heart started to beat at high speed. I felt scared to move. My heart felt heavier and heavier, like there was a heavy stone on it. What was more, I couldn't think straight. My body was frozen. The fear paralyzed me. I desperately wanted to hide.
>
> I kept the same position for almost two minutes. When the fear and the heaviness did not go away, I realized that it might be the presence of evil in the room. So I needed to make a choice: either I would keep my frozen position in fear until my parents came back or I would stand up and fight. I made up my mind: "If I die, I die. I don't want to be passive and doing nothing when Satan attacks."
>
> I ran into the kitchen and poured cooking oil into my palm. I started to say aloud, "Jesus' blood covers me and covers this apartment." I went to the door of each bedroom and used the oil to put a cross on the door while I was praying silently in tongues. I also prayed out loud: "This apartment belongs to Jesus. In Jesus' name, I cast out all the evil spirits and destroy Satan's work." I repeated this at each door.

---

3 Miller, *The Singer*, 69.

The last door I did was the main door. As soon as I finished drawing the cross on the main door and praying in tongues, my father opened the door from outside. He was surprised that I was standing so close to the main door. But I knew it was God's timing. The heaviness and fear in my heart were gone.

After this real experience, I was not as afraid anymore. I got used to running into the arms of Jesus and dared to face the oppression from Satan directly. I was telling myself, "Satan is the one who should be afraid of me, not the other way around. I have Christ's authority, which is more powerful than his. He should know I belong to Jesus and run away from me."[4]

For all believers, this confidence in Jesus's victory will be invaluable as they also confront evil in their settings. They need to know their identity and authority in Christ and learn how to recognize the presence of Satan. As Corrie ten Boom advises, "We need to recognize the enemy in order to overcome him. God wants and expects us to be conquering over the powers of darkness—not only for personal victory and the liberation of others' souls—but for His glory so that His triumph and victory over His enemies may be demonstrated."[5]

Therefore, in this book we will look first at how Jesus describes Satan, so we know whom we are fighting against. Then we will explore eight ways to claim the victory of Christ over all the various schemes of the enemy. "We would not be outwitted by Satan; for we are not ignorant of his designs," says the Apostle Paul (2 Cor 2:11 ESV). When we know how to fight back, then victory can be realized.

---

[4] Vivian Zhang, personal testimony, 2019.

[5] ten Boom & Buckingham, *Tramp for the Lord*, 72.

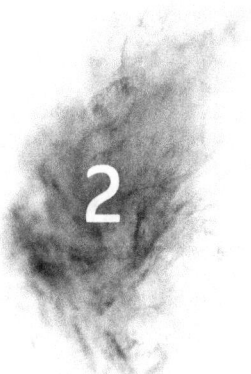

How Jesus Describes Satan

John Bunyan, author of another classic book *The Pilgrim's Progress*, described the biblical understanding of Satan perfectly. In one scene Satan has appeared to Christian, the book's protagonist: "Then Apollyon broke out into a grievous rage, saying [to Christian], 'I am an Enemy to this Prince; I hate his Person, his Laws and People; I am come out on purpose to withstand thee.'"[6]

In that effort to defeat all Christians, Satan uses three major approaches—as an *accuser*, a *liar*, and a *destroyer*. These are the very roles with which Jesus describes Satan's work.

Accuser

We see this accusing activity of Satan graphically in the Biblical scene in Zechariah 3, in which Satan is making accusations against Joshua the high priest. But God is present in this courtroom-style scenario, and God himself rebukes Satan in that encounter. Then God cleanses Joshua of his sin, gives Joshua clean clothes and a clean turban for his head and grants Joshua access to his courts. The progression is noteworthy. Satan's accusations of Joshua's sins are accurate. But God cleanses Joshua of those sins.

---

6 Bunyan, *Pilgrim's Progress*, 60.

At any point when Satan keeps accusing a Christians of guilt over sins confessed and forgiven, it is false guilt. White addresses this issue as well. He asks,

> How may I rid myself of the appalling burden of false guilt? How may I know the difference between the accusations of Satan and the convictions of the Holy Spirit? ... The long range answer has to do with Scripture. Day by day, week by week, year by year my conscience must be reinstructed, reoriented by a progressive knowledge of God's Word ... as practical experience is gained under the Spirit's tutelage. The Spirit convicts, the Enemy accuses. How may I know which voice is which? The Enemy seeks to destroy your fellowship with God. The Spirit, on the other hand, is attempting to restore your fellowship with God ... When sin is confessed, conviction will melt away and the blossom of fellowship will burst out with new fragrance.
>
> It also follows that if Satan is bent on destroying your fellowship with God and if your sense of sin results from Satan's accusation, then it will seem to you that your confession has somehow been inadequate, that you need to be more thoroughgoing in your analysis of your sin, more rigorous in your restitution. Yet to your dismay the confession is never thorough going enough.[7]

By using false guilt Satan makes the wrong assumption that those sins remain to disqualify Christians of their right to be in God's presence. But Satan's theology is faulty. When we become a Christian, God exchanges our sins for Christ's righteousness. It is being clothed in Christ's righteousness that enables us to be confidently in God's presence. The "breastplate of righteousness" is part of Christ's armor against Satan and will be discussed later in this book. What believers have to do is to remember

---

7 White, *The Fight*, 61–62.

this transaction of God on their behalf and thus rebuke Satan's attempts at accusation that God has already addressed.

Liar

As a liar, Satan works in three areas. First, he causes believers to doubt God's goodness and right motives. To Eve, in Genesis 3:4–5, he said, "You will not surely die. ... For God knows that when you eat of it your eyes will be opened, and you will be like God, knowing good and evil." Satan was trying to convince Eve that God was holding something back from her. Similarly, he lies to believers today about God's promises to protect us and guide us, causing us to fear the future.

Second, Satan lies to believers about their worth and God's love for them. He can cause us to doubt our salvation or forgiveness. He can cause us to doubt our ability to do what God says. Charles Kraft says,

> I believe that Satan attacks us primarily in the area of self image. He is desperately afraid we will discover who we are and make life difficult for him ... The devil often bluffs us and often wins because we do not know who we are... Satan does his best to keep us from confidently believing in the authority that God gives us. He wants us out of the race sidelined by our doubts, fears and weaknesses, it is up to us to accept the truth of who we are [in Christ] and to operate on it. God's Spirit does live within us no matter how we feel and the Spirit in us is more powerful than the spirit in those who belong to the world (1 John 4:4). God's truth is God's truth we need to believe it in the depths of our being. We need to speak it out to let the enemy know, we know who we are and then we need to act on it.[8]

---
8 Kraft, *I Give You Authority*, 154–55.

And third, Satan will lie about circumstances. He will cause a believer to focus just on what the culture says is possible or impossible and thus distort the reality of what God can make happen.

One Japanese international student who returned to Japan from the US experienced this distorted perspective. From a cultural perspective, things were made to seem impossible because God's power was taken out of the picture. It caused her great discouragement.

> I saw a Christian counselor/professor, whom I have known for seven years, in hopes of knowing more about the job of a counselor or a faculty position in Japan. She told me that jobs are scarce and it's hard to be a faculty member at a college. Overall, I felt discouraged. I think, in Japan, people generally tend to think "You can't do this" and "It's impossible." It's very disheartening.
>
> I also feel that the Japanese people tend to think that age limits us from doing various things. This might be my interpretation, ... but I feel more pressure of age here than in the US. In the US, I feel that I can do many things, if not everything. But in Japan, I feel that I can't do what I thought I could do in the US. Being in Japan might be making me become more realistic; but I can't really dream, and I have no one who can dream with me. [9]

Discouragement never comes from God. It comes from the lies Satan reinforces either from within the believer or from others in the culture—lies that most often slander God's character and expressed purposes of good for the believer. God says, "I know the plans I have for you, ... plans to prosper you and not to harm you, plans to give you hope and a future" (Jer 29:11).

---
[9] Miyuki Asada, interviewed June 24, 2018.

Destroyer

In addition to being an accuser and a liar, Satan is a destroyer. Peter describes him as "a roaring lion looking for someone to devour" (1 Pet 5:8). Jesus told Peter that Satan wanted to destroy him: "Satan has asked to sift you as wheat" (Luke 22:31). Satan purposes always to "steal and kill and destroy [God's people]" (John 10:10). Jesus told Peter, "But I have prayed for you, Simon, that your faith may not fail. And when you have turned back, strengthen your brothers" (Luke 22:32).

Jesus's prayers always bring victory against Satan. That surety can be a great encouragement for new believers: Jesus "has their back." No matter what methods Satan uses to try to destroy believers, Jesus's prayers are stronger and will prevail.

Still, it is important to understand Satan's various methods of destruction, including suicidal thoughts, unbearable guilt and shame, and all manner of unresolved woundedness. Sometimes that destruction wins, as it did for Judas, who hanged himself because he realized "I have sinned ... for I have betrayed innocent blood" (Matt 27:4). Other times Satan's destructive forces wreak long-term havoc in one's body and spirit.

Satan's purpose behind all these tactics is to "*wear down* the saints" (Dan 7:25 NASB) The NIV translates this same verse with the phrase "*oppress* [God's] holy people." Oppression creates a spirit of heaviness, a sense of powerlessness, and hopelessness.

Yet the heaviness of oppression is not only emotional heaviness. African Bible commentator Tokunboh Adeyemo says,

> Oppression comes as blasphemy, political injustice, social harassment, economic deprivation, and physical ridicule and

torture. Some or all of these tactics are used in persecution of believers today, especially in the Muslim world.[10]

These tactics cause compassion fatigue, a wearing down of one's soul, spirit, and body as things important to them get taken away—health, relationships, security, money, and jobs. Compassion fatigue can wear down the soul and the body because one's emotions so often get assaulted by the strains of persecution and torment, strains that can tend to go on unabated for long periods of time.

---

[10] Adeyemo, "Daniel," in *African Bible Commentary*, 1003.

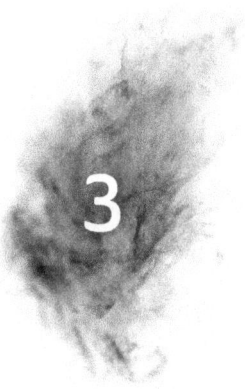

Eight Ways Believers Can Win Victory against the Enemy

But Satan's strategies are not the last word. Jesus came and died to defeat the power of the enemy. Colossians 2:14–15 says:

> Jesus canceled out every legal violation we had on our record and the old arrest warrant that stood to indict us. He erased it all—our sins, our stained soul—he deleted it all and they cannot be retrieved! Everything we once were in Adam has been placed onto his cross and nailed permanently there as a public display of cancellation.
>
> Then Jesus made a public spectacle of all the powers and principalities of darkness, stripping away from them every weapon and all their spiritual authority and power to accuse us. And by the power of the cross, Jesus led them around as prisoners in a procession of triumph. He was not their prisoner; they were his! (Passion Translation)

The eight ways believers can claim Christ's victory as their own are to:

1. Submit to God
2. Put on God's Armor
3. Resist the Enemy
4. Quote Scripture
5. Sing and Praise
6. Pray as a Prayer Warrior
7. Claim God's Ability to Demolish Strongholds
8. Wrestle in God's Strength

1. Submit to God

We start with James' admonition in James 4:7–8: "Submit yourselves, then, to God. Resist the devil and he will flee from you. Come near to God and he will come near to you." We can't resist the schemes of the enemy until we first submit to God. Submitting to God means humbling ourselves before God and declaring our utter dependence on him.

As long as we are in charge of our lives, we work in the flesh; we are driven by pride; we seek control of our future because we think we know best what we need. Pride is so natural to us, it is like the water we drink. Researchers call our pride the "Lake Wobegon Effect"—from Garrison Keillor's fictional Minnesota town where "all the children are above average":

> Psychologists call this the state of "illusory superiority." It simply means that we tend to inflate our positive qualities and abilities, especially in comparison to other people. Numerous research studies have revealed this tendency to overestimate

ourselves. For instance, when researchers asked a million high school students how well they got along with their peers, none of the students rated themselves below average. As a matter of fact, 60 percent of students believed they were in the top 10 percent; 25 percent rated themselves in the top 1 percent.

You'd think college professors might have more self-insight, but they were just as biased about their abilities. Two percent rated themselves below average; 10 percent were average and 63 percent were above average; while 25 percent rated themselves as truly exceptional. One researcher summarized the data this way: "It's the great contradiction: the average person believes he is a better person than the average person. ... We assume the worst in others while assuming the best in ourselves."[11]

Submitting to God also means being fully surrendered to God so that our unforgiveness, doubt, lust, anxiety, and sadness are replaced by forgiveness, faith, purity, love, peace, and joy. Submitting to God is making ourselves completely open for the Holy Spirit's transformation of our mind and character. This is the goal of Christian discipleship.

Finally, submitting to God means believing God can do miracles—through us or around us. It involves expecting to see God open a door of opportunity when no door exists. A Chinese international who came to the US to join his wife, who was pursuing her PhD, decided to take an additional master's at her university. However, he applied for the master's program after the deadline had closed! Amazingly, God opened the door and he got in. He was not a believer, but he recognized that as God's work.

---

11 ABC News, "Study: Self-Images Often Erroneously Inflate," November 9, 2005.

Similarly, I was accepted into the PhD program at Northwestern University even though the advisor told me to apply elsewhere for a DMin (Doctor of Ministry). He didn't think I could combine academic studies and ministry, and he told me there was no faculty advisor for my areas of PhD study. Both his premises proved false. I did complete my PhD at Northwestern, in only three years—while still doing ministry—and God provided four different faculty supervisors for the four disciplines in my PhD work. It was God's miraculous provision, equipping me to fulfill my calling.

Remember Peter's story in Acts 12? This is another story of God's miraculous work. Peter was in prison, bound to two Roman soldiers the night before he was to be executed. King Herod had already killed James. But the church was praying fervently for Peter. That night while the church prayed, an angel appeared in Peter's cell; the chains fell off his wrists; the guards were evidently put in a deep sleep; the prison doors and gates opened, and Peter walked to freedom. Ironically, the church had trouble accepting that miracle when Peter first showed up at the door. But even with their doubting faith, God worked. Submitting to God means being available for God to do miracles (and then believing them when they happen!).

However, an *unsubmitted* area is Satan's playground. Ego can convert anything to its own use, so Paul tells the Ephesians to deal with their anger issues immediately so that the sun doesn't go down on their wrath, because that gives an opportunity for the devil (Eph 4:26–27). Submitting to God means doing all God asks you to do when he asks you to do it and not allowing your own flesh to keep you from God's purposes. Corrie ten Boom calls this "Closing the Circle":

Eight Ways Believers Can Win Victory against the Enemy

If a Christian walks in the light (1 John 1:7–9) then the blood of Jesus Christ cleanses him/her from all sin, making her life a closed circle and protecting her from all outside dark powers. But if there is unconfessed sin in that life, the circle has an opening in it—a gap—and this allows the dark powers to come back in, ... Jesus has closed the circle with his blood so when we confess our sins, his blood cleanses us from all sin. I wish I could say that the circle has remained closed in my life. It is not so. For since Satan comes against us so often, it is necessary to confess often. And to ask forgiveness of others when we have sinned in their presence and grant forgiveness when someone asks to be forgiven. It is as important to forgive as it is to ask forgiveness. To withhold forgiveness often leaves another person in bondage, unable to close the circle and thus open to Satan pouring in many dark thoughts.[12]

2. Put on God's Armor

Paul told the Ephesians to resist the enemy by standing against the powers of evil in God's armor. Actually, all the other ways to gain victory over evil are based on this command of Scripture in Ephesians 6:10–17:

> Finally, be strong in the Lord and in his mighty power. Put on the full armor of God, so that you can take your stand against the devil's schemes. For our struggle is not against flesh and blood, but against the rulers, against the authorities, against the powers of this dark world and against the spiritual forces of evil in the heavenly realms.Therefore put on the full armor of God, so that when the day of evil comes, you may be able to stand your ground, and after you have done everything, to stand.

---

12 Corrie ten Boom & Buckingham, *Tramp for the Lord*, 170–72.

Stand firm then, with the belt of truth buckled around your waist, with the breastplate of righteousness in place, and with your feet fitted with the readiness that comes from the gospel of peace. In addition to all this, take up the shield of faith, with which you can extinguish all the flaming arrows of the evil one. Take the helmet of salvation and the sword of the Spirit, which is the word of God.

The armor of God includes "the word of your testimony"—the Word of God that has been proven true by you in your experience and about which you may legitimately testify. Once you are able to say, "the Bible says _____ and it was such a help to me that it really solved my problem," then the gates of hell will not prevail against you.

Putting on the full armor of God is not optional for a victorious Christian life. Every morning when believers start their day with God, they need to deliberately put on each piece of this armor. The helmet of salvation will protect their mind from the lies of Satan that distort reality and the character of God. The helmet of salvation will also protect the mind from the accusations from Satan that seek to shame and debilitate us. The breastplate of righteousness reminds us that Jesus is our righteousness and will defend us.

The shield of faith is to quench all the fiery arrows of the evil one. So often we don't even recognize those arrows, but when we put on the shield of faith, the promise is that *all* the arrows will be extinguished. Then we put on the belt buckle of truth, upon which we attach the sword of the Spirit so we will be able to say, "it is written, it is written, it is written." And finally, we put on the shoes of the gospel of peace so that we can go wherever God wants to take us that day. This is the daily clothing of the victorious Christian, so that we are not fighting the evil powers naked.

Corrie ten Boom uses another analogy that makes this truth very practical. She calls it the "Ding-Dong Principle":

> Up in a church tower is a belfry where bells are rung by hand by a rope that is pulled from the vestibule of the church... Yet, after the sexton lets go of the rope, the bells keep swinging. First "ding" then "dong", slower and slower until there is a final "dong" and it stops.[13]

I believe the same is true of deliverance. When the demons are cast out in the name of the Lord Jesus Christ or when sin is confessed and renounced, then Satan's hand is removed from the rope. But if we worry about our past bondage, Satan will use this opportunity to keep the echoes ringing in our minds. We can remember our old sins, they are the "dings" and the "dongs" of our past. When we hear them, we need to remember that through Jesus's sacrifice on Calvary, Satan can no longer pull the rope in our life. We may be tempted, and we may even fall back occasionally, but we have been delivered from bondage of sin.

3. Resist the Enemy

Clothed in God's armor, we can effectively resist the enemy, but that is a choice of the will. It takes courage and the confidence of victory—a confidence which the Holy Spirit can supply. It requires an attitude of readiness. In his sermon entitled "Courage," preacher Mark Buchanan gave this illustration:

> A few years ago at a Willow Creek Summit, Jack Groppel, who works with leaders to hone optimum performance, showed two

---
13 Buckingham, 179–80.

video clips. The first video was of a group of NFL linebackers. When they showed up for some training at Groppel's center in the swamplands of Florida, Groppel had an assignment for them: all the linebackers were to run to the perimeter fence of the center, either fetch a ribbon from a post or tie a ribbon to a post, and then run back to base camp.

Groppel then added one final, important detail: a wild boar had been spotted in the forest that morning. He explained how dangerous wild boars can be and how all the linebackers needed to be on high alert.

Off they went. In preparation for the activity, a cameraman had been planted along the forest trail, hiding behind the bushes. When you watch the video of what took place that day, these massive linebackers come around the bend looking panicky. At that point the cameraman begins to snort and rustle the bushes. The football players each turn tail and run, squealing like schoolgirls.

Then Groppel showed another video clip. It was of the same training scenario, only this time it's with CIA operatives. At the point where those operatives come around the bend and the alleged wild boar starts snorting and rustling, each operative gets into combat position and holds his ground.[14]

They were alert to the danger but had learned the importance of choosing to resist the fear and the "enemy" obstacles with courage in battle. Believers must refuse to be discouraged and pray against the tactics of discouragement and a seeming lack of fruit in our own and others' lives. We come against Satan's mind games, called psy-ops in warfare. Tim Downs, in his book *Head*

---
14 Buchanan, "Courage."

Game, explains:

> Psy-ops stands for Psychological Operations. An early example of this can be found in the battle strategies of Alexander the Great. On one occasion when his army was in full retreat from a larger army, he gave orders to his armorers to construct oversized breastplates and helmets that would fit men 7 or 8 feet tall. As his army would retreat, he would leave these items for the pursuing army to discover. When the enemy would find the oversized gear, they would be demoralized by the thought of fighting such giant soldiers, and they would abandon their pursuit.
>
> Satan likes to play head games with us, too, often leaving us demoralized by fear or doubt. We assume Satan is bigger or greater than he really is. The quickest way to thwart our enemy's psy-ops is to gaze upon the greatness of our God.[15]

4. Quote Scripture

The way Jesus resisted Satan was to quote Scripture—"it is written ... it is written ... it is written" (Matt 4:1–10). Believers need to be urged to memorize Scriptures that affirm God's power and greatness. Reciting Scripture is one way to push back the enemy. Revelation 12:10–11 says that "For the accuser of our brothers, who accuses them before our God day and night, has been hurled down. They overcame him by the blood of the Lamb and by the word of their testimony." Here are a few Scriptures to memorize as the word of a believer's testimony:

- God, my Rock—Psalm 18:1–3, 17–18
  The Lord is my rock, my fortress and my deliverer. ... He is my shield and ... my stronghold. I call to the Lord, who

---
15 Downs, *Head Game*, 309.

is worthy of praise, and I am saved from my enemies. ... He rescued me from my powerful enemy, from my foes, who were too strong for me. They confronted me in the day of my disaster, but the Lord was my support.

- God, my Shelter—Psalm 31:21, 19-20
  Praise be to the Lord, for he showed His wonderful love to me when I was in a besieged city. ... How great is your goodness which you have stored up for those who fear you. ... In the shelter of your presence you hide them from ... the strife of tongues.

- God, my Deliverer—Psalm 34:4
  I sought the Lord and he answered me; he delivered me from all my fears.

- God, my Purpose—Psalm 57:1-2, 7, 9-10
  I will take refuge in the shadow of your wings until the disaster has passed. I cry out to God Most High, to God who fulfills his purpose for me. . . My heart is steadfast, I will sing and make music among the people. ... For great is your love, reaching to the heavens; your faithfulness reaches to the skies.

- God, my Victory—Psalm 108:13; 109:31
  With God we will gain the victory and he will trample down our enemies. ... He stands at the right hand of the needy, to save them from those who condemn them.

- God, my Song—Psalm 118:6, 13-14
  The Lord is with me. I will not be afraid. ... I was pushed back and about to fall but the Lord helped me. The Lord is my strength and my song. He has become my salvation.

Eight Ways Believers Can Win Victory against the Enemy

We answer Satan's accusations, doubt, discouragement, and defeat with Scripture. When Satan brings doubt, our answer is 2 Corinthinans 1:18–22—"All the promises of God are yes in Christ" or Hebrews 6:18—"In Christ we can pull down strongholds and bring every thought captive to Him." When we fall and are defeated, our answer is that Jesus prays for us (see Luke 22:32 or Heb 7:25). And Micah 6:8 says: "We will arise and the Lord will be a light uno me." When we are discouraged and our hands hang down, our answer is Psalm 16:8—"I set the Lord always before me, I will not be shaken" or Romans 15:13—"the God of hope will fill us with all joy and peace in believing."

My Story

In mid-August of 2022, during a very difficult time, I felt besieged by the presence of the enemy. God brought a song to me called "How Firm a Foundation Ye Saints of the Lord." I described it in a sermon I sent out in August called "Sustained by the Power of God's Word." Here are the relevant highlights from that sermon that illustrate this principle of resisting Satan's attack by standing on our firm foundation of God's Word:

> Often God uses a song or a poem to make his truths real in our lives. That was my experience this week. Many of you know the difficulties of Keith's [my husband] journey through Alzheimer's disease for several years. An incident became acute these past two weeks so we had to move him out of his current Memory Care Center back home while we looked for a more suitable location for him. God never left us in our struggles, but Keith's agitated Alzheimer behaviors continued, Satan

was attacking me because I was working on a book, and I became exhausted.

But on Wednesday morning I awoke singing, *"Fear not, I am with you. O be not afraid, for I am your God and will still give you aid. I'll strengthen you, help you, and cause you to stand, upheld by My righteous, omnipotent hand."* I realized it was the words to the old hymn "How Firm a Foundation." It is actually a classic hymn from 1787 that is still in most contemporary hymnals today. As I read through all five verses, I realized this hymn summarized all God has done these many weeks and so it is the framework for my sermon this week. Here are all the verses: (If you recognize it, sing along as you go over the stanzas.)

1. "How firm a foundation, you saints of the Lord, is laid for your faith in his excellent Word.

2. What more can he say than to you he has said, to you who for refuge to Jesus have fle?

3. Fear not, I am with you. O be not afraid, for I am your God and will still give you aid. I'll strengthen you, help you, and cause you to stand, upheld by My righteous, omnipotent hand.

4. When through the deep waters I call you to go, the rivers of sorrow shall not overflow; For I will be with you in trouble to bless and sanctify to you your deepest distress.

5. When through fiery trials your pathway shall lie, my grace, all sufficient, shall be your supply. The flame shall not hurt you, I only design your dross to consume and your gold to refine.

Eight Ways Believers Can Win Victory against the Enemy

6. The soul that on Jesus still leans for repose, I will not, I will not desert to its foes. That soul though all hell should endeavor to shake, I'll never, no, never, no, never forsake!"

I believe we can claim these truths in spiritual warfare in terms of the problems of life, the promises of God, and the praises as we watch God fulfill those promises for us.

The hymn describes life's problems as:

- deep waters
- rivers of sorrow
- deep distress
- the fear of being overwhelmed
- fiery trials
- experiencing the pain of a refining process in Christian character
- foes who oppose Christians trying to live out God's plans for people, nations and the future
- and, all hell which endeavors to shake Christians from their committed walk in partnership with God and in fellowship with one another (often in storms, we tend to isolate ourselves and thus cut off our life support system)

That's a pretty all-encompassing list! And there are sometimes very concentrated periods when these problems seem to converge in our lives all at once and threaten to undue us. They are part of Satan's strategy to "oppress or wear out the saints" (Dan 7:25). Satan uses exhaustion, doubt, depression, discouragement, hopelessness, and defeat—any strategy to "steal and kill and destroy" God's people and purposes (John 10:10). Alzheimer's disease is one method Satan uses to achieve those goals. As Keith's wife and caregiver, that is a strategy Satan uses against me. But, as the hymn says, Jesus's sustaining power is greater and this hymn celebrates Christ's victory—all based on the sure foundation of God's Word.

Here are God's promises listed from the hymn:

- God is our refuge.
- God's Word is a sure foundation to build our lives upon.
- God promises to be with us, strengthen us, help us and cause us to stand upheld by his righteous, omnipotent hand.
- God supplies us with all-sufficient grace.
- God makes sure the flames from fiery trials do not burn us. He will bring us through.
- God will bless us in our troubles and sanctify us in our distress.
- God promises never to leave us nor forsake us.
- God will never desert us to our foes (which come against us in force to defeat us in the storms).

Let me unpack the promise of the firm foundation of God's Word as the umbrella concept behind all the other promises. It brings to mind the parable Jesus told of the two men who built houses—on the sand and on the rock. Most of us who have gone to a beach with children have experienced making marvelous sandcastles. My kids did it with moats and turrets and the whole shebang! But when the tide came in that sand masterpiece disintegrated pretty quickly. However, Jesus says when you build your house on a rock—a *firm* foundation—the waves can crash against it and winds can beat upon the house but it will not fall because it has its foundation on a rock. We build our lives on the Rock when we hear Christ's words and put them into practice! Amen. (Matt 7:24–25) This is why we study and memorize Scripture. It is our investment and guarantee that God will be our protector; God will be our sustainer; God will keep us from being destroyed by all the battering storms that come our way. God will bring us through. God will bring us through.[16]

5. Sing and Praise

A fifth way to fight against the heaviness of oppression is by claiming the Messiah's promise in Isaiah 61:3 that the Messiah gives believers "the garment of praise in place of the spirit of heaviness" (KJV). Believers need to put on that garment of praise when evil surrounds them. An Indonesian international student tells this story:

> I was out on a camping trip with some of my friends from college in a village in Java Island, Indonesia. The first night two of my Christian friends and I went for a walk to a nearby community center just to explore the village area. On our way back to our tent at 7 p.m., it was dark and the three of us were chased by a dog. As we walked farther from the community center, more dogs joined the circle to chase us. They barked

---
16 www.maryloucodmanwilson.com, preaching series, 8/7/22.

at us as if they were ready to attack and bite us—like we were a thief or a ghost. Dogs are known for being able to sense the presence of evil spirit or ghosts. I remember how terrified we were. We joined hands and walked together like a pack of three. I could sense there was something wrong; it was like evil spirits were playing around us. I had creeps and goose bumps, which I rarely had even when I was being told a ghost story.

Because we were terrified, I sang a Sunday school song in Indonesian: "Dalam Nama Yesus," which means "In Jesus' Name." The song goes "In Jesus' name, Satan will be defeated." My friends were praying out loud to Jesus for protection. We were all scared. Thankfully, the dogs who were following us were just barking as they surrounded us.

We arrived at our place safely, although our bodies were still shaking from the terror. Later that night we learned that there was a girl in the area who was possessed by a demon, at the same time we were chased by the dogs. The dogs were responding to the evil they felt. But the evil spirits were not able to get into us because we have Jesus. I felt that there's power in Jesus' name through praise songs![17]

6. Pray as a Prayer Warrior

John White says,

> Prayer is not you trying to move God. Prayer is among other things being caught up into God's directions and activities. He orders the affairs of the universe, and he invites you to participate by prayer. Intercession is God and you participating in partnership, bringing his perfect plans into being.[18]

---

17 Hanny Wuysang, interviewed July 21, 2018.
18 White, *The Fight*, 15.

Eight Ways Believers Can Win Victory against the Enemy

Wesley Duewel, in his book *Mighty Prevailing Prayer*, agrees:

> The prayer warrior stands between the authority and power of heaven and the darkness and power of hell, between the Lamb on the throne and Satan, the Great dragon. Christ has delegated to the prayer warrior his authority, the right to use His name and plead His blood (Rev 12:11). The prayer warrior is to enforce the victory of Calvary on the battlefield of earth.
>
> Prayer is a militant force that has the potential of defeating Satan, destroying his works and driving him out of places and lives he claims for his own. ... You must repeatedly call his bluff, reaffirm and insist on Calvary's victory and force his vacating all he has so arrogantly usurped.[19]

Duewel adds:

> The New English Bible translates James 4:7 *"Stand up to the devil and he will turn and run."* ... The Greek literally says "oppose." This is a command. You do not defeat Satan by passively "looking to the Lord."
>
> The command to take a stand against Satan, to resist and oppose him, is as much a command as the command to witness or to preach the gospel.
>
> Our world is a battleground. ... Calvary was planned by God not only to deliver us from our sins but to empower us so that we can defeat Satan. God the Son defeated Satan at Calvary and depends on us now to enforce His victory by prayer warfare.[20]

---

19 Duewel, *Mighty Prevailing Prayer*, 233, 235.
20 Duewel, 242.

The role of prayer warrior, as seen in the verbs "enforce," "plead," "defeat," and "drive out," shows the believer's critical participation in enforcing Christ's victory. As Duewel notes, "you do not defeat Satan by passively 'looking to the Lord!'"[21]

7. Claim God's Ability to Demolish Strongholds

In our prayers, we need to claim 2 Corinthians 10:3–5:

> For though we live in the world, we do not wage war as the world does. The weapons we fight with are not the weapons of the world. On the contrary, they have divine power to demolish strongholds. We demolish arguments and every pretension that sets itself up against the knowledge of God, and we take captive every thought to make it obedient to Christ.

Satan works through the strongholds in our minds and society. But believers have divine power in Jesus Christ to "take captive every thought to make it obedient to Christ" (2 Cor 10:5). We can "be strong in the Lord and in his mighty power" (Eph 6:10). The Greek word here that is translated "be strong" is *endunamoo*—"to empower, enable, increase in strength." *Kratos*, "in his mighty *power*," means "power, vigor, domination, and strength." The Greek word translated "mighty" is *ischus*, meaning "forcefulness and ability."

Not only that, but we take down Satan's strongholds "by the blood of the Lamb and the word of our testimony" (Rev 12:11). Claiming the covering of the blood of Jesus protects believers from evil's destructive power—much like the lamb's blood applied to the Israelites' doorposts in Egypt protected them from the angel of death.

The word of a believer's testimony can be a Scripture verse that is relevant in the particular battle he or she is facing. In the

---

21 Duewel, 242.

face of the evil accusation that "suffering is the final word," the testimony may be: "Our God, the God of all comfort, reigns" (2 Cor 1:3–5; Rev 19:6). When people fear abandonment, believers can claim Jesus's promise, "Surely I am with you always to the very end of the age" (Matt 28:20). In times of financial distress, the testimony word could be, "And God is able to make all grace abound to you, so that having all sufficiency in all things at all times, you may abound in every good work" (2 Cor 9:8 ESV). When there are cascading worries, the testimony word may "cast all your anxieties on him because he cares for you" (1 Pet 5:7).

As the Holy Spirit brings the appropriate Scripture to mind, converts can claim that Scripture as the word of their testimony and stand on God's victory. I cannot stress enough how important this is in actually pushing back the power of the enemy in our lives, our churches, our families and our world.

8. Wrestle in God's Strength

Finally, the Apostle Paul likens such a stand against Satan to a wrestling match. He says, "For we wrestle not against flesh and blood, but against principalities, against powers, against the rulers of the darkness of this world, against spiritual wickedness in high places" (Eph 6:12 KJV). We pray, we stand, we rebuke, we push back against the reality of those forces and claim Christ's victory over them. That is prayer in Christ's authority. Duewel says:

> We will be astonished to realize the scope and intensity of the prayer battles all across the church as it faced the world and its need. ... Heaven fights with us as we prevail in prayer. We are prevailing with God and for God.[22]

---

22 Duewel, 237.

To avoid their loss of faith when converts return to the Far East, they need to claim these eight ways to overcome the enemy so that their Christian life can thrive and they can withstand all the ways Satan tries to discourage, depress, and defeat them. Christ has won our victory. We need only to stand in it. And praise God for it!

Bibliography

Buchanan, Mark. "Courage." Preaching Today. https://www.preachingtoday.com/sermons/sermons/2009/june/courage.html.

Bunyan, John. *Pilgrim's Progress*. Penguin Classics, 2009.

Downs, Tim. *Head Game*. Nashville: Thomas Nelson, 2007.

Duewel, Wesley. *Mighty Prevailing Prayer: Experiencing the Power of Answered Prayer*. Grand Rapids: Zondervan, 2013.

Hesselgrave, David J. *Communicating Christ Cross-Culturally*. Grand Rapids: Zondervan, 1991.

Kraft, Charles H. *I Give You Authority: Practiving the Authority Jesus Gave Us*. Grand Rapids: Chosen Books, 2012.

Miller, Calvin. *The Singer: A Classic Retelling of Cosmic Conflict*. Downers Grove: InterVarsity Press, 2020.

ten Boom, Corrie with Jamie Buckingham. *Tramp for the Lord: The Hiding Place*. New York: Jove Books, 1978.

White, John. *The Fight: A Practical Handbook for Christian Living*. Downers Grove: InterVarsity Press, 1976.

Get Involved

Every book in the Snapshot Series is created to give you an overview of a subject that really matters and to provide reflection questions and ideas that will help you move to action.

Learn—For more information, visit www.maryloucodmanwilson.com.

Connect—Reflection questions for you and/or a group:

1. What are your experiences with the spirit world?

2. In what practical ways can you strengthen your spiritual life to practice the eight keys to victory?

3. How do Corrie ten Boom's two analogies of the "Closing the Circle" and the "Ding-Dong Principle" help you practically as you deal with Satan's strategies?

Do—Be encouraged because we have victory in God! Review the eight ways believers can claim Christ's victory as their own. Pick one out to focus on this week. Reread that section and ask God how you can grow in effective spiritual warfare.

1. Submit to God
2. Put on God's Armor
3. Resist the Enemy
4. Quote Scripture
5. Sing and Praise
6. Pray as a Prayer Warrior
7. Claim God's Ability to Demolish Strongholds
8. Wrestle in God's Strength

Also by Dr. Mary Lou Codman-Wilson

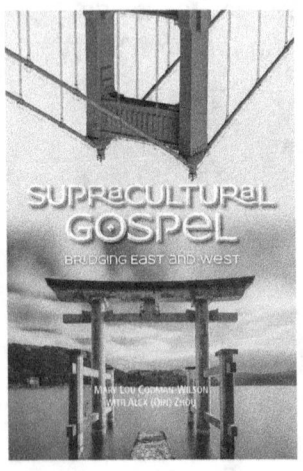

Supracultural Gospel: Bridging East and West

Join Drs. Mary Lou Codman-Wilson and Alex Zhou as they dialogue about Alex's experience becoming a believer in the US and his struggle to share his faith when he returned to China. They model a process of examining our cultural worldview to overcome the tensions associated with living out our faith in a context dominated by different religious or secular systems. *Supracultural Gospel* presents: seven principles to adapt the gospel to bridge East and West; essential attitudes and practices of emotionally healthy and spiritually discerning discipleship; and key gospel concepts in non-Western terms, while retaining biblical accuracy.

Written in a highly conversational tone and validated with personal stories from many Asian internationals, *Supracultural Gospel* is a powerful and practical tool for those who are passionate about cross-cultural discipleship.

Visit us at missionbooks.org

www.ingramcontent.com/pod-product-compliance
Lightning Source LLC
Chambersburg PA
CBHW071256070526
44583CB00017B/2488